NI

CW00569947

NIKKI

It has taken me 5 years to write this book, the insights of my alcoholic father, the love affairs of my family members, domestic violence, child abuse & broken homes.

This was my childhood and the truth of my trauma.

"I'm sorry."

TABLE OF
CONTENTS

CHAPTER 1
The Truth

Craig Jones, an alcoholic from Tyne and Wear, was the child of Loretta and Christian Jones. He had two stepbrothers named Trevor and Stewart. Craig did not have the best start in life; when he was just five years old, his mother abandoned him and his stepbrothers, which left them to be brought up by Derek, Craig's stepfather.

Craig was a very troubled child; he was kicked out of numerous schools for his inappropriate behaviour.

Derek was getting to his wits end when he read in the newspaper about a boarding school in Northumberland for troubled boys. Derek then believed it would be in Craig's best interest to enrol him in the boarding school.

Craig joined the boarding school in September of 1991 when he was just 12 years old. He started to really fit in with the other children, made a lot of great friends, his behaviour drastically improved, and found he really enjoyed physical education.

After a few months, Craig started rebelling out of the blue and occasionally escaped from the boarding school. After each time, he was returned, but little did anyone know what horrors they were returning him to.

In February of 1992, Craig had escaped from the

boarding school once again and ran to his mother's home, where he was greeted by Stewart. He then burst into tears and begged to not get sent back. For months, Craig kept a terrifying secret: he was being sexually abused by his PE teacher. When Stewart confronted him with the accusation, Craig explained that other teachers knew, but they brushed it under the rug as Craig wasn't the only one this was happening to. Unfortunately, Loretta did not believe her son, so she sent him back and ignored his cry for help.

This abuse lasted for nearly a year; during this time, Craig turned to alcohol as a coping mechanism.

In July of 1992, Derek found out about Craig's drinking

from the headteacher at the boarding school. He decided to bring Craig back home to live with him and his two stepbrothers to try and get him some help. Craig did not want to tell Derek about the abuse he endured because he believed there would be no point, as he thought no one would believe him if his own mother didn't.

Derek was now a single parent to three children in a two-bedroom home in Cramlington, Northumberland.

Upon Craig's return, Derek realised just how out of control Craig's drinking was. From the moment he woke up to when he went to sleep, he always had some cider in his hand. When he was getting drunk, he would get very violent with anyone who tried to ruin his 'fun.

Because of Craig's anti-social behaviour in the neighbourhood, they were evicted from their home in Cramlington and moved to Walker, Newcastle, in 1993.

In Craig's teenage years, his behaviour was getting worse; he started stealing money from Derek, leaving the family with little to no money each month. In light of this, Derek decided to start his own business as a window cleaner to have a more suitable income for his family.

CHAPTER 2
Love Affair

Derek was finding it quite difficult to find regular customers. There was a lot of competition in the area, but he was still optimistic about finding more customers. Derek confided in his son Stewart, and quite quickly Stewart noticed just how much they were struggling.

One summer night, Stewart was out with friends when they bumped into a girl named Kim.

Kim Brown, born in Newcastle, is a daughter to Carol and a sister to Taylor and Charlie.

Stewart and Kim started dating the moment they met. Upon meeting Stewart, he was a very open book and told Kim about his dad's business and how it was suffering. Kim then told Stewart her mother would have some business for him as their window cleaner recently retired.

The next day Derek went to visit Kim's home to discuss becoming the window cleaner. Kim's mother opened the door to Derek, and it was love at first sight. However, there was just one problem: Carol was married.

Derek was working every week at Carol's home. He noticed he could be going once every two weeks, but he was enjoying her company too much. Each time he was offered a cup of tea with some biscuits after he was finished the windows, along with having deep conversations with Carol. They had grown a wonderful friendship; Derek was falling in love with her, and he knew Carol and Frank didn't love each other, so he started hoping for some luck.

A few weeks later, he decided to invite Carol to celebrate his 40th birthday with him after he had finished work. She jumped to the offer; she hadn't been out in weeks, and she would work all day every day with two jobs to keep the roof over her children's heads. That night, Carol and Derek were having a great time. The pub started closing, so they decided to go back to Derek's flat for more drinks, as it wasn't too far from the pub. They had a wonderful night, and to Derek's surprise, Carol admitted she had feelings for him. They knew what they were about to do was wrong, but they ended up making love anyway.

During the whole week after, Carol couldn't stop thinking about Derek and the night they spent together. She knew she had to confess to Frank and then decided to leave him, they didn't love each other anymore. She walked out of the family home and went to Derek's. Derek was absolutely ecstatic; he couldn't believe she actually left Frank for him.

A week later, Carol was told by a friend that Frank had left, so she decided to go home and invited Derek, Craig, and Trevor to move in with her, as she knew how much they were struggling. Derek agreed, but they knew they had to break the news to all of their kids, especially Kim and Stewart.

When breaking the news to Kim and Stewart, they were annoyed, but they decided to split so their parents could have a relationship, as it would just make everything complicated, and they only wanted their parents to be happy.

Craig had envied his stepbrother for being with Kim; he fancied her for a while, but there was an age gap of three years. He was overjoyed when he found out about Stewart and Kim breaking up and decided to take his shot with Kim. Craig approached Kim in the kitchen when no one was around and started being very flirtatious. He then asked her if she wanted to start dating, but it would have to be their little secret. Kim felt very flattered, as she found him very attractive. She knew it was wrong, but the excitement took over, and she agreed.

Unfortunately, their secret relationship didn't last long when they were having sex in Kim's bedroom, Derek had come home, but they didn't realize it. Derek heard the sexual noises, went upstairs, opened the bedroom door, started screaming at them both, and decided to kick Craig out of the house. Because they were caught, they decided to break it off publicly but continue to keep it a secret. However, this time the breakup had to seem more convincing, so they decided to also start seeing other people.

Two years later, in 1998, Craig was with a woman called Maggie, whom he was dating for a while, and he made the decision to move into her mother's home. Kim visited Craig at Maggie's home while she and her mother were out, but she was distraught as she found a pregnancy test on the bedside table... Maggie was pregnant.

While confronting Craig about it, she noticed he smelt like cider, which isn't an unusual smell for him, but she then noticed he smelt like that all of the time.
She also asked him about the cider, and she found out about Craig's alcoholism. Kim was so angry; they were meant to stop being a secret in less than two years. When she turned eighteen, it was all planned. How could he do

this to her? It was their future, and now it's all ruined. With her anger, she decided to leave Craig and let him have the family she wanted.

Kim went back home after seeing Craig she was heartbroken, but she didn't want to break up a family. She started throwing up, and while throwing up, she noticed her period hadn't come that month. She ran down to her mother's medical cupboard and took out a pregnancy test, hoping it would just be because of how sad she was. Unfortunately, it wasn't; she was pregnant.

Kim started panicking; she couldn't be a single parent. How would she tell her mom and Derek? She wanted to keep the baby, but as she didn't believe in having an abortion, she had to come clean.

When Carol returned home, Kim was sobbing on the sofa with the pregnancy test in her hand. She knew exactly what happened and knew who the father was, she was her mother after all.

Kim decided to keep the baby with Carol's support, although she was still only sixteen. She knew it was going to be difficult; people would stare and have opinions, but she had everyone she needed around her to help bring up her child. In a very difficult decision, Kim didn't want to tell Craig she was pregnant until she had the baby, as she knew he would leave Maggie, and she didn't want that to happen.

CHAPTER 3

When It All Began

On January 30, 2000, I was born, weighing six pounds and half an ounce. For my mother, her pregnancy was very healthy, labour went smoothly, and my nanna Carol supported her all the way through. My dad was informed I was born; however, he didn't want anything to do with me as he had his own family now.

After giving birth to me, the nurse suggested my mom get a wash while she was waiting for my nanna to return from getting food. She didn't want to leave me alone, but the nurse insisted. She asked the nurse not to give me my bottle as it would be my first feed. When she was finished with her shower, she came out of the bathroom, and to her horror, the nurse was feeding me. She went absolutely crazy, screamed at the nurse, and said, "She's your baby now." My mom then got her stuff and left me in the hospital.

My nanna came back to notice my mom was gone, and the nurse told her what happened. I was discharged, and my nanna took me home, where upon our return, my mom was already there.

The first six months of my life, my nanna was bringing me up. It was very difficult for my mom; she knew she had something wrong with her as she couldn't feel the love she wanted to feel, found herself having a lot of guilt, and felt like her motherly instincts weren't going to appear.

appear. She decided to get some help, and she went to see a psychiatrist and was diagnosed with postpartum depression, which was very difficult for her. She did try her best to keep involved with me, such as by feeding me, changing my nappies, and holding me, but she just wasn't feeling any different.

Her psychiatrist suggested she may need to move out of the family home, and that could help with our bond, so she did, and we moved into a flat in Slatyford, Newcastle.

A month passed of us living there, and my mom's postpartum depression was improving. She was able to love me more and more each day, and she was feeling a lot less guilty for leaving me in the hospital.

The same month she had a knock on the door. It was my dad; he had come to try and reconnect with her. He told her he left Maggie; he had slowed down on his drinking; and he wanted to be a family and to meet me for the first time. She was still so much in love with my dad, so she decided to give it a go.

But the happy home was soon to be my mom's worst nightmare.

My dad was still drinking every day and started taking money from my mom's purse, which was for my essentials. She found out and spoke to her psychiatrist for some advice. The psychiatrist stated he should go to rehab because of how long he had been drinking along with some therapy.

When the day's session was finished, my mom returned home to find my dad slumped and absolutely plastered on the sofa. She then proceeded to settle me in bed and put me in her bed for the night. She went downstairs, and my dad was awake, pouring himself another drink. "Do you not think you've had enough, Craig? Why don't we get ourselves up to bed with the bairn as she will wake up soon anyway?" My dad then looked at my mom with a facial expression she had never witnessed before, but it sure wasn't going to be the last time. He then proceeded to get up and stumble over to her. "Don't you dare tell

me when I've had enough? I say when I've had enough."
He then clenched up his fists and started punching her
multiple times in the sides, then her legs, then her arms,
she was curled up like a baby trying to protect herself.

He stopped. She lay there still, so confused about what
had just happened. What did she do? Did she say
something to upset him? Maybe she provoked him? She
stood up and went to bed, sobbing, and just cuddled me
the whole night, hoping he wouldn't come in.

The next day, my mom got up with me to make my
morning porridge, but still, with so many questions
going through her mind from the night before, she was
adamant it was her fault and she shouldn't have told
him

what to do. The floors creaked from upstairs, and my dad was getting up. Her heart sank; she just hoped he was in a better mood. She scurried to me in my high hair and proceeded to feed me. The sitting room door opened, and he entered in hysteria and threw himself onto his knees in front of her. "Kim, I'm so sorry. I don't know what got over me. Please forgive me. You know I love you. It won't ever happen again. I swear down on the bairns life and on my ma's life. Please, Kim, will you forgive me?" "Yes, Craig, I'm sorry too." She then hoped it was just a one-time thing, but surely he mustn't have meant to hurt her when he was this upset? How wrong she really was.

Two days later, as always, my dad was drinking on the

sofa, I was crying as I was due my feed, and my mom was in the kitchen finishing making the bottle and putting it in a jug of cold water to cool down. "Will you shut up that bloody bairn!" My mom's heart started racing as she grabbed the ice out of the freezer to try and cool the bottle quicker. "Yes, I'm sorry; I'm just trying to cool her bottle, Craig. I'm sorry, I'm doing it as fast as I can." He threw himself off the sofa, stumbled into the kitchen, and shouted, "You're not doing it quick enough, then, are yi?!"

My mom recognised his face from two days prior and immediately shielded her face, only to feel the blows of my dad's fists again and again and again until he stopped and left the house. My mom dropped to the floor in tears and thought maybe she should've had it ready for my

feed time; maybe she wasn't doing it quick enough.
After around an hour, my dad returned, begging my
mom for forgiveness, but this time blaming it on me for
why he was so tired, my mom forgives him again.

Every day for four months, this was my mom's reality;
no one else knew about it as my dad would hit her in all
the hidden places. Police were called by the neighbours
numerous times, but they couldn't do anything as my
mom kept telling them everything was fine and it was
just an argument, but the neighbours knew; they heard
my mom's screams and her crying; they had enough.

One night they tried intimidating my dad as they were
worried about my mom, and they couldn't bear to listen
to it anymore because they threatened him and told him

they heard it all. He ended up thinking about what my mom told them; even though she didn't say a word, he was paranoid. So that night, he hit her again, and her screams continued, but this time the neighbours ran down, kicked the door in, and started pouring petrol all over the flat. My mom was screaming, "My baby! My baby!" She grabbed me and ran out of the flat, with my dad following to my nanna's.

My nanna was shocked when my mom and dad came through the door. My dad had told my mom she better not say anything or he would kill her, so she made up a story about the neighbours being psychopaths, and it was actually them who broke in as I was crying.

My nanna was very sceptical; she knew something didn't add up, so the next day she sent Derek, Taylor, and

Charlie to go and question the neighbours and teach them a lesson.

Upon them leaving, my dad dragged my mom to the bedroom and said, "You know they're going to find out! I'm going to go to prison! If I can't have you, no one can!" He threw his hands around her neck and started strangling her. She was trying her best to get him off her, so she started stamping on the floor and hitting the wall as hard as she could. Luckily enough, my nanna was downstairs with me, and she heard the banging. She ran up the stairs, burst into the room, and immediately grabbed onto my dad and ripped him off my mom. He turned around and bit her on the shoulder to make her let go, then ran as quickly as he could out of the house before anyone returned.

My mom knew then she had to come clean and tell the truth about her nightmare over the past few months, and my nanna assured her it wasn't her fault; she had done nothing wrong, to never take him back, and it wouldn't happen again.

CHAPTER 4
Hide & Seek

Months later, my mom was petrified of my dad returning; he knew where she was, so she decided to move into her own place. She found a flat in Wallsend that we had moved into, but it was suddenly cut short when she found the flat was covered in insects the night we moved in. She called the council, and they told her an exterminator would be out in the next two weeks. My clothes were covered in insects, as was all of our furniture. It was just getting worse as the days went on.

In desperate need, my mom moved us into a private rented house in Forest Hall, which was owned by an elderly couple. However, my mom didn't realise it was a temporary contract as the elderly couple wanted to sell the house. My mom was feeling frustrated, so she contacted the council, who stated that once she received the notice for us to leave, they would rehouse us.

The council contacted my mom and told her they had a flat we could move into. Upon viewing, my mom loved it, and we moved in the same day.

After a few weeks, my mom had been suffering from PTSD. Unfortunately, she shortly realised we had a drug dealer move in above us. He was selling all sorts of illegal drugs and allowing people to go into his home and get high. My mom was terrified as her PTSD was taking over due to all the fighting, shouting, and people opening the block door, she believed my dad would find us, so she put in for another move on the basis of her mental health. She had to inform the council that the loud noises of other people around her were causing her PTSD episodes, as she couldn't tell them she had a drug dealer living above her as she wouldn't be a snitch.

My mom was so deflated. I was coming up to two years old, and she wanted me to start nursery, but all the thoughts going through her mind were making everything worse. Will my dad find us and kill her? Would she ever be okay again? Would she ever find a suitable place for us to call home?

The following month, the council contacted my mom and

informed her they had a property for her to view that day in Walker, she rushed over hoping that this would be the one. She fell in love; it was perfect—two bedrooms, very spacious, a large front and back garden, as well as just along the road from a primary school that enrolled children from the age of 3 into their nursery.

Our perfect family home had finally been found. My mom was working so hard on our home to make it perfect with the little income she had. My mom gained a wonderful friendship with the neighbours, Johnny and Celine; they had a son who was around the same age as me, which connected them more.

She confided in Johnny and Celine about the stress she

had trying to find a home and opening up about her relationship with my dad and how he abused her. They were both very supportive but also comforted my mom about how strong she was and that she had actually been a survivor of domestic violence.

One day, there was a knock at the door. Upon opening the door, my mom froze. My dad had found us. He confidently just walked into the house upon making eye contact with me, picked me up, and turned to my mother with a smirk on his face. "Hello, long time, no see."My mom was frozen, and all she could hear was her heart pounding in her chest. She calmly sat down on the sofa and looked at my father. "What do you want, Craig? What are you doing here?" "Came to see my girls, ain't

I? Hya' i'm sorry Kim, I've got help, I'm not drinking any more, propa sorted myself out, wor mush helped get my life sorted, I kna I shouldn't have raised my hands, will yi forgive me? Gis' another chance, aye? I will make it up to you." She believed what he was saying to be true; he didn't smell of drink; it had been a while; maybe he was telling the truth? She still loved him very much and really hoped he had changed.

They spoke for a while, and when she went to go make a cup of coffee, she noticed there was only a little bit of milk left. She nervously asked him to watch me while she popped next door to get some milk, and he agreed with no issue, no argument, and no attitude. She was relieved and really believed he had changed.

The door opened immediately. "Eeee, who's that lovely bloke in ya house?" Celine was known to be the nosey neighbour. "It's Craig; have you got any milk I can lend till I get to shop tomorrow?" Celine then looked at my mom, shocked. "Why are you letting him in? Aye, I've got milk for you, but do you not want me to call the police? Kim, you shouldn't be letting him in." Sharply, my mother replied, "I didn't let him in; he just walked in, he says he's changed; he's not going to hurt me again; he's stopped drinking; and everything, Celine, I believe him." Celine grabbed the milk for my mom, then softly grabbed her hand. "Leopards never change their spots; I'm here if you need me, but please think about you and that bairn, you're not alone." My mom grabbed the milk, gave Celine a hug, and then returned home.

For the next year, everything was fine; my dad was still drinking, but he didn't raise his hands to my mom. When he didn't have a drink, he was the most amazing dad and partner. It was coming up to my third birthday, and she was so happy to finally have me start school later in the year.

Just before my third birthday, it was a normal day, but my mom and dad were arguing about my birthday presents, she didn't have a lot of money because she realised he had been taking money from her purse again. She then felt a very familiar pain she felt before; he punched her in the back of the head and screamed, "Well, if you just got rid of her, we wouldn't have an issue!" She immediately turned around and dragged him out of the house with all the strength she had, locked the door, and told him to never come back.

The next day, my mom took me to my nanna's house. I always stayed one day every week. I absolutely loved my nanna, but my mom was scared my dad was going to come back. She told my nanna what happened the following night and asked if it was ok for me to stay so she could sort herself out. My nanna agreed but was very concerned about my mom, so she confided in Stewart and asked him if he would pop over to check up on her and make sure everything was okay.

Stewart went to check on my mom that night. He realised she was very emotional, so he decided to make them some coffee and sit with her for a while. He was comforting my mom, something she hadn't had for a while. They were laughing, and it was the first time in a long time my mom didn't feel as scared. One thing led to another, and they ended up having sexual intercourse. They both instantly regretted it, and Stewart swiftly left, along with my mom, feeling awful about what just happened.

Six weeks later, my mom went to the doctor, as she had flu-like symptoms that weren't going away. Upon her visit, the doctor decided to do a pregnancy test as they couldn't figure out why she wasn't getting better, but there was a reason: she was pregnant with Stewart's baby. Unfortunately, Stewart wanted my mom to get an abortion; she wasn't meant to fall pregnant, and it wasn't expected from anyone, but my mom decided to go along with the pregnancy. Four weeks before my mother's due date, she went into premature labour.

On March 12, 2004, my little brother, Aiden, was born.

CHAPTER 5
What I Can Remember

My mom was enjoying being a single parent, although it was hard. She built herself a routine with me being four years old and my brother being a baby. My life was great with just my mom and Aiden; I loved my little brother; I was really enjoying school; I had made a lot of friends; and I was learning very quickly.

After school, my mom collected me as always with Aiden. I was skipping home while getting closer to my front gate. I then noticed my dad perched on the doorstep, waiting for us. My dad was sober. He stood up and said to my mother, "Let me see the bairn for a bit. Can we talk?" My mom just nodded and unlocked the door and let him in. He was great with me and Aiden; he helped my mom with making bottles, changing Aiden's nappy, and playing with me. They spoke in the kitchen away from us, and the next minute I knew my dad was staying.

That day, me and my dad went to his flat in Byker to get some of his belongings. I was so thirsty, so I went to the fridge, and it was full to the brim of cider cans, and there was a small bit of milk left. I opened the lid, and the stench of off milk flew up my nostrils, making me vomit. I put it back and proceeded to sit on my dad's sofa while he was collecting his things, then we went home.

A few days later, my mom didn't turn up to pick me up

so Celine took me back home; the door was unlocked, and my mom was sobbing on the sofa with my dad mumbling in the kitchen. He then came through to the living room shouting, "I told you to get the bacci, that bloody child of yours. Now I'm gon' have to get our bacci, Nikki, are you wanting to come with da?" I nodded in fear of getting shouted at.

We then left the house and got the bus to an area I had never been to before. It was a large cul-de-sac of flats. My dad shouted up to someone's flat, and they popped out the window, throwing a bag down with tobacco in it. Upon getting to the other side of the cul-de-sac, the police showed up, stopping next to us. The police officers rolled the windows down, looking at my dad. "Craig, what are you doing around here? You know you're not meant to be here." My dad picked me up, replying, "Aye ana I'm just getting bacci for the missus and I'm going straight back now." The police officers stopped the engine and got out of the car "Craig you know we can't let it slide" my dad held me tighter. "Ah, haway man, I'm going back; please not in front of me bairn just take us back if yis' don't believe me." "Sorry Craig," the police started saying a lot of things I didn't understand while taking handcuffs out of their belts. I then felt someone's hands on my sides and started screaming, clenching onto my dad as much as I could. The police officer snatched me off my dad. I was screaming so scared at everything going on. "Daddy, please, that's my daddy; please don't take him away from me; he's not been bad; please, daddy, no!" They threw my dad in the back of a police car, all while knowing I was witnessing it all, then put me in the back of another. I was scared; I didn't understand what was going on. I just remember seeing my mom at the front door with Aiden in her arms. The police spoke to my mom and explained he had been arrested as he had a restraining order out for the area where we picked up the tobacco, and my mom knew the order was from his ex-girlfriend Maggie.

The next day, my mom took us to so many police stations and courts, we couldn't find him anywhere, and no one was telling her anything. We went back home, and my mom told me he would be back soon, but in reality, she didn't know; no one knew if he would be returning anytime soon.

My dad didn't return till a week later. I was so relieved to see him and ran up to him, giving him a massive hug, but I was still so confused about why the police took him away. I asked him, "Why did the police get us, daddy? You weren't being bad." My dad instantly replied, "Police aren't good, Nikki; I'm a good man; they are bad people; they took you away from your dad; don't forget that." I nodded, but I was still so confused. I had thought the police were meant to help you, not make you upset.

Months following I kept hearing my mom and dad argue every day. I knew my dad was drinking and noticed that when he would drink, he would get angry, so I kept out.

of his way. I heard the abuse my mom got, the connections of my dad's fists to her body, and her screams for him to stop. I would hide under my covers every time I heard him coming up the stairs and pretend to be asleep.

On a Saturday, I was getting ready to go to the neighbour's house, and I asked my mom, "Why does daddy hit you, mammy?" She replied calmly, "Oh, darling, daddy only smacks mammy's bum when she's being naughty; he doesn't hit me, okay?" I knew sometimes I got a smacked bum if I was misbehaving, so I nodded. I didn't realise my dad was in the kitchen, and at the time I didn't have any pants on. "Why are you asking so many questions? Get your bloody trousers on now!" He threw my trousers off me and started stumbling towards me. He was drunk. "CRAIG!" My mom screamed, and the next minute I knew I had excruciating pain in my face and fell to the floor. My dad had slapped me. I burst into tears, threw myself up, ran up to my room, dove on my bed, and hid under my covers. I was so scared. Why did he do that to me? I hugged my rag doll in hysterics: "My daddy is a bad man; he just hit me on my face, it hurts." I cried and cried until I eventually fell asleep.

I didn't realise my mom kicked my dad out that night. When I woke up, I quietly went downstairs when I heard my mom on the phone say, "No, Craig, you can hit me or even kill me, but you will never raise your hands to my kids. Never, do not come back, or I swear down, I will get you arrested. You will never see her again, do you hear me?" I knew she was on the phone with my dad, and I had a sense of relief knowing he wasn't there.

My mom got us ready, and we went to the council office for an emergency move. She told them everything, and there were police reports of suspected DV but nothing verifying it. They agreed to give us an emergency move, but they also contacted social services to try and keep us away from him.

When returning home, my mom was packing our belongings as the council called, stating they would be moving us the next day and they had a property available. My mom took us next door to say goodbye, and Celine turned to my mom softly with tears, "I told you leopards don't change their spots; don't ever turn back now, for those kids, look after yourself, Kim." My mom nodded and hugged her, and we went back home to continue packing.

That night my mom was still packing the last bits in the kitchen before going to bed when she got a fright from someone banging on the window. Someone was standing there with a knife. She froze and grabbed a knife from the draw, then realised it was my dad and his friends terrorising her with ski masks on. One minute they were at the window, one minute at the door, and they were making her so frightened. "You can run, but you can't hide, Kim. I will find you; I always do." My mom just fell on the floor in hysteria; she couldn't do it anymore, but after a few minutes later they left. My mom called my uncle Charlie out of fear that my dad and his friends would come back. He came straight over and woke me up. "Come on, let's go for a sleepover at nanna's." I was so excited but confused because of how dark it was outside. I loved staying at my nanna's, but why were we leaving at night?

The next morning, my mom went back home to meet up with the moving van to get our stuff and go to our new home. Once my mom was finished at our old home, I was collected from my nanna's and we moved into a maisonette in Throckley, which was on the other side of Newcastle.

Hoping my dad wouldn't find us, my mom knew we were

hiding again, but we didn't realise that this would be the

last time we would ever need to hide from my dad.

CHAPTER 6
New Beginnings

I was staying at my nanna's, which was just down the road from our new home, while the decorating and main moving were being done. My nanna took me up to see the progress of the maisonette, and when I got there, I realised there was a lot of carpet on the balcony. "Uncle Charlie, make me a tent, please!" My uncle Charlie giggled and made me a carpet tent. I got into it all excited, looked down from the balcony, and saw two other girls, one brunette and one blonde, playing with their doll prams and shouted, "Bang bang, got you!" The girls looked up and giggled. "Are you moving into that new house?" I replied, "Yes, I am." The girls then asked, while my mom was coming to the door, "Do you want to come and play with us?" I looked at my mom, so excited, and she nodded with a soft smile. I ran down the cement block stairs and met them at the exit. "Hi I'm Nikita!" The blonde replied, "I'm Kalie, and this is Ali. Do you want to be our friend? I only live over there, and Ali lives over the road." Kalie pointed to the other maisonette on the right side of the field. I nodded with a huge grin on my face. From that moment on, I knew I would have some great friends. We played for hours, talking about the area, and I found out I was going to be at the same school as them, which was right next to the masionettes. I was so excited.

The first day of school, I was very nervous. The teachers were lovely, and I was welcomed by everyone.

While on lunch break, I looked over and saw a man at my door posting a letter, so I assumed it was a postman. I was having a wonderful first day at school. Meanwhile, at home, my mom noticed the letter that came through the door; it was handwritten and didn't have a stamp on it. She opened it, and it was a letter from my dad. He had written how he was sorry, he wanted contact with me, he stopped drinking, and all the rubbish she heard from him in the past, she scrumpled up the letter and threw it in the bin.

At the end of my school day, I walked home with Kalie and Ali. I was so lucky to have such good friends. I was enjoying my new life so much that I had forgotten about the past year. When I got home, my mom had food ready and I told her all about my day; she was so pleased, and it seemed to really calm her. I finished all of my food, tidied my bedroom, then went and played outside with Kalie and Ali.

On bonfire night 2006, my dad came banging on the door and said, "Kim let me in! I want to see Nikki; she needs to know how sorry I am. I want to make it up to her. Let her come out and see the display. I have bought loads of fireworks, Nikki! Dad's here; do you want to come see the fireworks I have got for you? Haway, darling!" I just hugged my mom tightly in the sitting room. "No, Craig, don't you understand she's scared of you? Just go away before I ring the coppa's." A few minutes later, I went up to my room and looked out my window. My dad had set up a huge display, let off the fireworks, and started leaving the field. I was so relieved when I saw him walking away.

The following week, my grandad Derek took myself and my cousin Natasha to see my uncle Riley. We were having such a great day with my grandad on the buses; we loved our bus trips. We had to get two buses to see my uncle; upon getting on the second bus, we were only ten minutes away until we had to get off, when my dad got on the bus with his new girlfriend Katie. I froze; my heart was thumping out of my chest; all I could hear was background noise, then the hands of my grandad picking me up and passing me to my dad. "NO, NO, PLEASE NO!" I was shrieking so loudly that I popped my ears. I was petrified. "Nikki, it's da haway, darling, calm down." I looked at his smile on his face and said, "You are not my dad! I hate you, and I wish you were dead!" He swiftly put me down, and I'm positive that if the bus didn't have other people on it, I sure would've felt his anger again. I ran to my grandad, fell to the floor still in fear, and wrapped my arms around his legs as tightly as I could. My dad then got off the bus and waved goodbye. "I love you, Nikki."

After we got off the bus, I just wanted to go home. I just needed to feel safe. On the bus home, all I could think about was that I did hate my dad, but I also loved him; he was my dad after all. When we got home, I ran to my mom and gave her a hug.

My grandad explained what had happened, my mom was furious, and from that day on, my grandad wasn't allowed to take me out alone again.

CHAPTER 7
Kim's Saviour

In 2007, my mom had been a single parent for two years. She was ready to start dating again. My mom didn't want anyone local, as she couldn't bear to have the pity of what everyone knew. Throckley is a small village, so everyone knew each other's business. So she decided to start phone dating. She had a lot of weirdos to start with—men just wanting a one-night stand or they were already in relationships.

She then started talking to a man named James, from Sunderland. I would hear her laugh and talk for hours late at night. I had never heard her laugh the way she did with him. Anyone could tell just how happy he was making her, but at the same time also scared. After six months of talking to James, my mom wanted him to meet us. She sat me down and explained that he was coming over for tea after school. I agreed, but all I could think of was, What about my dad? Is James going to beat my mom up?

Later that day, I finished school and walked home with my friends. When I walked into my home, all I could smell was a mix of Jimmy Choo perfume and spaghetti bolognaise. I peeked around the kitchen door, and my mom looked so beautiful. Her hair and make-up were done, and it was the first time in forever I had ever seen her dolled up.

Then there was a knock at the door. My mom opened the

door to this muscular, tall man with long, dark hair and dark eyes. "Well, aren't you a sight for sore eyes?" He kissed my mom on the cheek, and she welcomed him in. He had a gentle smile. "Hi I'm James, and you must be Nikita?" I nodded. I wanted to smile or answer back, but I just couldn't; he seemed nice enough. My mom shouted, "Foods ready, kids," We sat down to eat; I was on the single chair, Aiden on the floor, then my mom and James on the sofa.

James was trying very hard for me to make conversation with him; he even tried showing me his long hair, which had plaits in it, and said, "If you're ok with it, I can show you how to plait hair." I bluntly replied, "No, it's ok; my mom can show me; you're not my dad." Sharply, my mom finished her mouthful of food. "Nikita! Don't be so rude, he wasn't saying he's your dad; he's just trying to be nice." "Well, he isn't my dad and never will be; I'm full!" I stormed away, put my dish on the bench, and went up to my room. Why was this man being so nice? He was trying to be my dad, wasn't he? I didn't want anyone in our lives. I liked my life just the way it was.

James was coming over and staying every weekend from Friday to Sunday. I hated it. After around six months, I found out he proposed to my mom, and she said yes. I was furious. Why wasn't I asked first? I knew I would've said no if he asked, but it still wasn't the point.

The wedding wasn't long after the proposal; it was a

beautiful wedding, not a big wedding, as we didn't have a lot of money, but we all had a lot of fun. My mom looked stunning, and even I thought James looked charming at the ceremony. At the wedding, my mom sat down with me and said, "I know he's not your dad, but he makes me very happy. You don't have to call him dad, and James is fine with that, but please, he is trying, darling." I sighed and looked at my mom with a desperate plea in her face. I knew she needed me to like him too. I wasn't sure if I ever would, but I looked at her and said, "ok mam, I'm sorry. I'm happy you're happy. I love you." "I love you too." She softly kissed me on the head and smiled.

After the wedding, I went and stayed at my nanna's

house. I was so excited. I absolutely loved staying at my nanna's; she would do puppet shows with a clothing rack and a towel, along with giving me a cup of hot chocolate before bed. It was wonderful; it was my safe space, and she was my safety net.

That night I heard my nanna and grandad talking; they weren't too certain on James; they wanted my mom to be happy, but it was obvious to everyone; they rushed into it. Also, with what happened with my dad, my nanna was vigilant about my mom getting into another relationship. While listening to the conversation, I was silently agreeing that I didn't want my mom to be with James.

The next few months were fine; I was the perfect

daughter to my mom, went to school, ate all of my food, tidied my room, played outside with friends, and returned when I was told. On the weekends, me and my mom would do some crafts and colouring, but I was not the best with James; I didn't like him and would avoid him as much as I could. When he came over at the weekend, I always felt he was getting between me and my mom, and this would cause arguments between me and him.

My mom was sick every morning; she went to the doctors and said she needed to speak to me after school, and I just knew what she was going to say. She was pregnant; I didn't want another sibling, as I knew this would make James come around more often.

On September 27th, 2009, my mom gave birth to my beautiful sister Alexis. I really enjoyed being a big sister again, nevertheless, I still didn't like the thought of James being around more, but I knew he was just trying to be the best dad he could, as well as being a stepdad to me and Aiden.

CHAPTER 8
The Moment Time Stood Still

Two thousand and eleven, the year I was leaving primary school, I was getting prepared to do my SATS. I was so excited to be going to high school. Kalie, who was a year older than me, had already started high school; she was my best friend, and I couldn't wait to be in the same school again. It wasn't the same not walking home with her, and our friendship had plummeted due to her having new friends and me not being the same age.

In March 2011, my grandad came to my home to speak to my mom. Little did I know that my mom had been in contact with social services, as my dad wanted contact. He had stopped drinking for three months and was in recovery, he had been in the hospital due to his pancreas failing and decided to stop drinking to save his own life.

Social Services had been given proof of my dad's alcohol levels while in the hospital, which showed he had stopped drinking, he was getting healthier, went to Alcoholics Anonymous, and sorted his life out. Once he felt ready, he contacted social services, and they agreed he could have supervised contact.

When my mom found out, she pretended the letter didn't come from social services and binned it. The day my grandad came, there were arguments, and all I remember my grandad saying was, "Do you really think she will be in danger? He's stopped drinking, Kim; the proof is there, he is her dad; he deserves to see her." I knew right away they were talking about my dad. I had mixed emotions; if he really stopped drinking, this would mean the hitting wouldn't happen again.

I walked into the kitchen and looked at my mom. "I want to see him, mam, please?" "I just don't know Nikita; what if he starts drinking again?" My grandad sternly butted in, "Well, then she won't see him again; if I smell one bit of drink on him, we will walk away, okay?" My mom paused, looked at me, then back to my grandad and replied, "Fine, but you are not to leave him alone with her; you have to be there every minute." My grandad nodded, and I hugged my mom and said, "Thank you."

Closer to the end of March, I was getting so excited, telling everyone I was going to see my dad. I was counting down the days, at my nanna's my grandad phoned my dad, and we spoke for around twenty minutes. I could tell he really had changed. Before ending the call, I said, "I love you, dad; I can't wait to see you next week." "I love you too, Nikki. I will get you a gift. See you next week." I was smiling from ear to ear. I just couldn't wait to see him again, but this time it would be different; he would be my dad and act like one.

I heard my mom and James having numerous arguments about me going to meet my dad. He was concerned he was going to worm his way back into her life, but my mom was reassuring him it wouldn't happen. I was secretly hoping it would; if my dad was better, why couldn't we be a family again? I wanted my dad, not James.

On Friday, March 31, 2011, two days before I was going to see my dad, it was a normal day. I went to school, and at assembly, I got a golden award. These were awards for students who stood out to teachers, and it was the first time I ever had one. I was absolutely over the moon. My life seemed so amazing at the time. I was going to see my dad, been given a golden award. It couldn't have been better, and nothing could have ruined my mood that day.

After school, I ran home as quick as I could waving my golden award, like Charlie in the chocolate factory with his golden ticket. I ran up the stairs of our block, swung open my front door, and bounced into the kitchen,

I found my mom on the phone, "She's here now; ring you back soon." I then started screaming with joy, "MAM, MAM, LOOK, I GOT A GOLDEN AWARD. LOOK, MAM, WOO!" My mom looked at me softly with a small smile on her face. "That's great, darling. Put it on the fridge. I have to tell you something." Happily, I replied, "Ok, mam, but look at it look." "Nikita darling, please go into the sitting room; I need to speak to you." I looked at my mom, very confused about why she was being so serious, I could tell she had been crying. I wasn't ready for what was about to come. I put my award on the fridge and went into the living room, still full of joy and a massive smile on my face. I sat down, still fidgeting and moving around. My mom came in and kneeled in front of me. "I need you to listen to me, ok?" She looked at me in the eyes, held my hands tightly, and softly said,

"I'm so sorry, your dad is dead."

Printed in Great Britain
by Amazon